CREATION
BY DESIGN

by Mark Eastman, M.D.

P.O. Box 8000, Costa Mesa, CA 92628

Creation by Design

by Mark Eastman, M.D.
Published by **The Word for Today**
P.O. Box 8000, Costa Mesa, CA 92628
800-272-WORD (9673)
http://www.thewordfortoday.org

ISBN 0-936728-68-X

© 1996 The Word for Today

TABLE OF CONTENTS

PREFACE

When Luke wrote the message of the gospel to Theophilus, he declared that his desire was to set forth in order a declaration of those things that are most surely believed among us. Luke desired that Theophilus might know the certainty of those things in which he had been instructed.

We seem to be living in a day of spiritual confusion. Paul wrote to the Ephesians that they not be as children, tossed to and fro with every wind of doctrine by the slight of men and the cunning craftiness whereby they lie in wait to deceive. Because of all the confusion in the church today, and the many winds of doctrine that continue to blow through the body of Christ, we felt that it would be good to have various pastors write booklets that would address the issues and give to you the solid

1

biblical basis of what we believe and why we believe it.

Our purpose is that the spiritual house that you build will be set upon the solid foundation of the eternal Word of God, thus we know that it can withstand the fiercest storms.

Pastor Chuck Smith
Calvary Chapel of Costa Mesa, California

CHAPTER I

THE GREAT DEBATE

For since the creation of the world His invisible attributes are clearly seen, being understood by the things that are made, even His eternal power and Godhead, so that they are without excuse.

Romans 1:20

In the book of Romans the Apostle Paul expressed this fundamental biblical truth that the existence of God is obvious to all men.

3

According to Paul, the evidence for God's existence is found in the "things that are made," so that those who do not believe in God "are without excuse."

Until the middle of the nineteenth century, the prevailing world view, even among the world's university intelligentsia, was that the universe and its life forms were the result of intelligent design from a transcendent, supernatural Creator.

However, in the last 150 years an unparalleled shift in world views has occurred. At the end of the twentieth century, the biblical notion of a transcendent Creator is now ridiculed as an irrational, patently unscientific world view.

Incredibly, the Bible, and its view of creation, has been thrown out of the public schools in the United States. What was once the most revered book in the land, the first textbook in the first public school in America, is now treated as contraband by the scientific and educational establishments.

The seed for this remarkable shift in world views came in 1859 with the publishing of the book, *The Origin of Species*, by Charles Darwin.

In his book, Darwin sought to explain the origin of all life forms without the benefit of intelligent guidance or a supernatural act of creation. The millions of animal species on earth are, according to Darwin, the result of blind "descent with modification."

According to Darwin's theory, those organisms best adapted to their environment will compete more successfully for resources. Consequently, those organisms will be expected to live longer and pass those beneficial traits to the next generation. Those that are "less fit" will lose out in the competition for resources and die, thus failing to successfully pass their traits to subsequent generations.

According to Darwin's theory, over time these beneficial traits will accumulate in the population eventually resulting in the production of a "more fit" population. Over great periods of time Darwin envisioned the production of entirely new species through this random, piecemeal process.

On the surface, certain aspects of Darwin's theory seem reasonable. We know, for example, that prolonged isolation of a few animals of the same species can, due to inbreeding, result in a population that appears significantly different from the parent population.

However, in the last forty years discoveries in molecular biology and information theory have highlighted the numerous deficiencies in Darwin's theory and its modern formulation.

In the pages that follow we'll see that Darwinian theory is not only incapable of explaining the origin of complex systems, such as brains, hearts and the visual system, but also has no rational naturalistic explanation for the origin of life, which is absolutely necessary for evolution to act.

Indeed, apart from the minor variations seen among individuals of a breeding population, neo-Darwinian theory explains virtually nothing of the origin and diversity of the life forms on earth.

CHAPTER II

THE ORIGIN OF LIFE

It is often said that all the conditions for the first production of a living organism are now present, which could ever be present. But if we could conceive in some warm little pond, with all sorts of ammonia and phosphoric salts, light, heat, electricity, etc., present, that a protein compound was chemically formed ready to undergo still more complex changes.

Charles Darwin, 1859 Origin of Species

The question of life's origin has been debated by philosophers, theologians and scientists for thousands of years and is at the very core of the debate between the evolutionists and the creationists.

Indeed, without an explanation for the origin of life, the theory of evolution, with its non-theistic foundation, is dead in the water.

Darwin recognized that a purely materialistic explanation for the origin of life was foundational to the theory of evolution. To the evolutionary "purist" the introduction of a miraculous cause for life's origin "taints" the theory. Consequently, evolutionists have, since Darwin's *Origin of Species*, sought to explain the origin of life in purely chemical terms.

Evolutionists (non-theistic) assert that life arose by the fortuitous interplay of time, energy and chance chemistry, acting on non-living matter.

Creation scientists view the origin of life as a purposeful contrivance by an intelligent Creator who applied information or biochemical "know-how" onto matter at the time of creation.

These two world views can be expressed mathematically by the following formulae.

Evolution Formula

Matter + Energy + Chance Chemistry = Life

Intelligent Design Formula

Matter + Energy + Information = Life

In the evolutionary scenario, the origin of life represents the first step, i.e., the trunk, in the evolutionary tree of life on earth. However, it is at this point in the theory of evolution where the "rubber meets the road." For at this point, if the evolutionists cannot present a plausible naturalistic explanation for the origin of life, then Darwin's theory of evolution is dead before it enters the starting gate.

The Scope of the Problem

The question of life's origin is much more complex than just explaining the origin of the molecular machinery ("hardware") found in living cells.

Like a computer, living systems also require "software" or coded instructions to direct the activities of the cellular "hardware."

During the time of Charles Darwin the structure of the cellular hardware, and the system of information storage used by living systems, was unknown. However, when the structure of the DNA molecule was deciphered by James Watson and Francis Crick in 1953, a revolution in our understanding of cellular information storage began.

Watson and Crick discovered that the DNA molecule is formed by two strands of nucleotides (the chemical "letters" of the genetic code) which are twisted in the form of a double helix (see figure 1). The sequence of these chemical "letters" ultimately determines the structure and function of every organ in living systems.

Figure 1

DNA

Deoxyribonucleic
Acid

Nucleotides

A= Adenine

T= Thymidine

C= Cytosine

G= Guanine

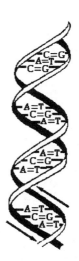

The DNA molecule is formed
by two chains of nucleotides
which are bonded together to
form the structure of a spiral
double helix. Somewhat like
a ladder which is twisted from
the top down.

Since 1953, molecular biologists have
concluded that the growth and metabolism of all
life on earth is carefully controlled by a digital,

error correcting language convention called "the Genetic Code" which is "carried" by the DNA molecule.

Any theory which attempts to explain the origin of life, in the absence of a Creator, must be able to explain not only the origin of the molecular hardware (DNA, RNA, Proteins etc...), but the enormously complex, coded information found in all living systems as well.

Spontaneous Generation

The evolutionist's scenario on the origin of life proposes that some four billion years ago, inanimate chemicals developed by chance into highly complex, living, single-celled organisms. It is generally believed to have occurred somewhere in a "primordial ooze," near deep, hot oceanic vents or in a shallow tidal pool. This process has been dubbed "Spontaneous Generation."

Spontaneous generation was first proposed in the sixth century B.C. by the Greek philosopher, Anaximander. He argued that life arose from mud when it was exposed to sunlight, and that it subsequently evolved into all life forms, including man.

The Modern Paradigm

In 1859, Charles Darwin revived Anaximander's theory and suggested that life had arisen in some "little pond" as a result of sunlight acting on various organic salts.

In the 1920's Russian biochemist, I.A. Oparin, and English biologist J.B.S. Haldane proposed that life had arisen from simpler molecules on the lifeless earth under much different atmospheric conditions than exist today.

They proposed that ultraviolet light, acting on a primitive atmosphere, containing water, ammonia and methane, produced oceans with the consistency of a "hot dilute soup" containing the building blocks of life.

In 1952, Harold Urey noted that most of the planets in our solar system, except earth, have an atmosphere which contains little or no free oxygen. Furthermore, Urey knew that the building blocks of life are quickly destroyed if they are exposed to an environment containing oxygen. Therefore, he concluded that spontaneous generation must have occurred on the early earth with an atmosphere consisting mainly of hydrogen, ammonia, methane, water vapor, but _little or no_ molecular oxygen.

Stanley Miller's Bombshell

In 1953, a graduate student named Stanley Miller set out to verify the Oparin-Haldane-Urey theory.[1]

Attempting to simulate the early atmospheric conditions, Miller passed a mixture of boiling water, ammonia, methane and hydrogen through an electrical spark discharge in a system of glass flasks. On his second attempt, Miller produced a mixture containing very simple amino acids, the building blocks of proteins.

The major product of Miller's experiment was tar (85%) and carboxylic acids (13%), both of which are toxic to living systems. In addition, small quantities of the amino acids Alanine (0.85%) and Glycine (1.05%) were synthesized. Trace amounts of the essential amino acids Glutamic acid, Aspartic acid, Valine, Leucine, Proline, Serine, Treonine were also produced.

Stanley Miller's experiment was seen by believers as virtual proof that organic chemicals, and ultimately life, could be produced by chance chemistry. It brought a greater measure of scientific respectability to the theory of spontaneous generation and evolutionary thought. Evolution, according to the purists, could now be taught as a virtual certainty.

The impact of this experiment on the scientific community is expressed by evolutionist and astronomer Carl Sagan:

> *The Miller-Urey experiment is now recognized as the single most significant step in convincing many scientists that life is likely to be abundant in the cosmos.*[2]

This opinion, however, is not universally held by evolutionists. With the advantage of four decades of hindsight, and extensive discoveries in molecular biology, the "spark and soup" Miller-Urey paradigm on the origin of life is now seriously questioned by world authorities.

Problems with Miller's Experiment

Since Miller's original experiment in 1953, a number of serious problems with the "spark and soup" paradigm have been highlighted by world authorities. The following is only a summary of some of the difficulties encountered.

Toxic Waste: The Cradle of Life?

The major products of the experiment (tar and carboxylic acids) are poisonous to living systems. Such chemicals poison and ultimately kill living systems by binding irreversibly to the protein enzymes in them. This is how modern pesticides kill their prey. In fact, had he drunk the solution his experiment produced, it is a virtual certainty that Stanley Miller would have died. To argue that such a toxic environment is the cradle of life requires a great deal of faith.

Secondly, these chemical by-products (tar and carboxylic acids) bond to the building blocks of life (amino acids and nucleotides) far more readily than they bond to each other! Consequently, it becomes an exercise in futility to believe that pure proteins and DNA could arise out of such a chemical quagmire.

Atmospheric Mythology

The atmosphere proposed by Oparin, Haldane and Urey was not arbitrary. It was absolutely necessary or else the building blocks of life could not be produced. Ammonia, methane and hydrogen gas are necessary to supply the carbon, nitrogen, hydrogen and oxygen in the building blocks of life. Without these atmospheric gasses a naturalistic explanation for the origin of life is doomed.

To the dismay of origin of life researchers, atmospheric scientists have, in the last 25 years, concluded that the methane, ammonia and hydrogen atmosphere would have been destroyed in a few thousand years by ultraviolet radiation. This is a woefully inadequate time to allow for spontaneous generation. Secondly, there is strong evidence that oxygen was abundant on the early earth. This means that the building blocks of life would be rapidly destroyed by oxidation before they ever reached the primordial soup. In fact, evidence now indicates that the early atmosphere was composed of carbon dioxide, water vapor and nitrogen gas.[3]

The Myth of the Primordial Soup

One of the foundational principles of spontaneous generation is that life arose in a body of water. Stanley Miller and his colleagues believed that the building blocks of life would be made by simple chemistry in the atmosphere and then fall gradually to the earth's bodies of water. There, the building blocks of life would combine into long chains of nucleotides and amino acids forming DNA and proteins respectively.

While on the surface such a scenario seems plausible, there is one extraordinary difficulty with the primordial soup theory. Water, the major component of the theoretical primordial soup, causes the chains of DNA, RNA and proteins to _break down_ into their individual building blocks.[4] This process, called hydrolysis, is now well known to origins researchers and is one of the greatest problems with the current paragigm.[5]

The Case of the Missing Letters

In the English language convention there are twenty-six letters that are used to write sentences, paragraphs, chapters and books. These letters are strung together according to hundreds of predetermined rules. Anyone with a knowledge of those rules can understand the information conveyed by the sequence of letters.

In every living system there is a special set of four chemical "letters," called nucleotides, which are used to "write" the information stored by the code of life, the Genetic Code. Millions of these nucleotides are strung together, end to end, in long chains, thus forming the DNA molecule (Figure 1). These chemical letters represent only a tiny part of the "hardware" that must arise by chance in order for spontaneous generation to occur. However, nucleotides are much more complex than the simple amino acids made by Miller and Urey, and would require much more chemical expertise to produce.

Many claims have been made that nucleotides of DNA have been produced in such "spark and soup" experiments. However, after a careful review of the scientific literature, evolutionist Robert Shapiro stated that the nucleotides of DNA and RNA;

> ...have never been reported in any amount in such sources, yet a mythology has emerged that maintains the opposite.... I have seen several statements in scientific sources which claim that proteins and nucleic acids themselves have been prepared...These errors reflect the operation of an entire belief system...*The facts do not support this belief...Such thoughts may be comforting, but they run far ahead of any experimental validation.*[6]

After nearly four decades of trying, with the best equipment and the best minds in chemistry, not even the "letters" of the genetic code have been produced by random chemical processes. If the letters cannot be produced by doctorate-level chemists, how can we logically assume that they arose by chance in a chemical quagmire?

Chirality: The Death Blow to Spontaneous Generation

One of the most devastating problems with the primordial soup scenario is the problem of chirality. The building blocks of DNA and proteins are molecules which can exist in both right and left-handed mirror-image forms (Figure 2).

Figure 2

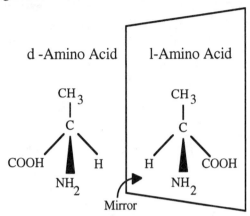

Levo and Dextro Amino Acids

This "handedness" is called "chirality."

The difficulty for any naturalistic explanation for the origin of life is that all "spark and soup-like" experiments produce a mixture of 50% left (levo) and 50% right-handed (dextro) building blocks. However, in all living systems DNA and RNA are composed exclusively of right-handed nucleotides, while the amino acids in virtually all proteins in living systems, with very rare exception, occur only in the left-handed form. The only known way to separate the two forms is with biochemical expertise! But this comes only from a mind.

Consequently, not only is "Primordial Soup" toxic to living systems, it is totally incapable of producing the pure "left-handed" proteins and pure "right-handed" DNA by chance.

Evolutionist Robert Shapiro comments on the significance of the Miller-Urey experiments:

> *The very best Miller-Urey chemistry, as we have seen, does not take us very far along the path to a living organism. A mixture of simple chemicals, even one enriched in a few amino acids, no more resembles a bacterium than a small pile of real and nonsense words, each written on an individual scrap of paper, resembles the complete works of Shakespeare.[7]*

The Odds

In the last 30 years a number of prominent scientists have attempted to calculate the odds that a free-living, single-celled organism, such as a bacterium, might result by the chance combining of pre-existent building blocks.

Harold Morowitz calculated the odds as one chance in $10^{100,000,000,000}$.

Sir Fred Hoyle calculated the odds of only the proteins of an amoebae arising by chance as one chance in $10^{40,000}$.

When you consider that the chances of winning a state lottery every week of your life from age 18 to age 99 is about one in 4.6 $\times 10^{29,120}$, the odds calculated by Morowitz and Hoyle are staggering.

These odds led Fred Hoyle to state that the probability of spontaneous generation "is about the same as the probability that a tornado sweeping through a junk yard could assemble a 747 from the contents therein."[8]

Mathematicians tell us that any event with an improbability greater than one chance in 10^{50} is in the realm of metaphysics-i.e., a miracle.

Origin of the Software

Shortly after the structure of DNA was deciphered, the method of information storage and retrieval used by living systems was quickly determined.

While the structure of the DNA molecule in and of itself displays no intrinsic information, it does, however, have the ability to "carry" or hold information, just like the ink in these letters or the iron atoms in a floppy disc can carry meaning or information.

Remarkably, the information on the DNA molecule is stored in a "digital" fashion, expressible in distinct mathematical terms.

In recent years molecular biologists have also discovered that the information on the DNA molecule is redundant. There are numerous genes (segments of DNA that code for the production of a particular protein) which occur in multiple places in an organism's genetic blueprint. Consequently, if one gene is damaged by mutations, the backup gene can take over the production of the necessary proteins.

Another fascinating aspect of information storage on the DNA molecule is that it is error correcting. When a DNA molecule is copied there are occasional errors in the placement of nucleotides, the building blocks of DNA. After the duplication of DNA, a protein moves along the newly produced "daughter molecule" and screens for copying errors. If an incorrect nucleotide is found, the correct one is placed assuring the purest possible duplication process.

Finally, evidence is accumulating that the information on the DNA molecule is overlapping! That is, there are segments of DNA that can code for the production of more than one protein!

Digital, error correcting, redundant, overlapping information storage systems—the products of chance? Hardly. They are the products of Ph.D's in information theory and computer science!

Encyclopedia on a Pinhead: Chance or Design?

At the moment of conception, a fertilized human egg is about the size of a pin head. Yet, it contains information equivalent to about six billion "chemical letters." This is enough information to fill 1000 books, 500 pages thick with print so small you would need a microscope to read it! If all the DNA chemical "letters" in the human body were printed in books, it is estimated they would fill the Grand Canyon *fifty times!*

The information on the DNA molecule is transferred to RNA and ultimately to proteins in the form of structural and functional proteins.

A fundamental dilemma for the evolutionary theory is that the duplication and translation of the information on the DNA molecule requires the employment of proteins. However, living cells cannot make proteins until the DNA replication and translation machinery is in place!

The only rational explanation for this dilemma is that the protein production and DNA replication and translation machinery system arose simultaneously! This could only happen by design.

The Nature of Information

In the previous section on the origin of the cellular hardware we presented abundant evidence which mitigates against the spontaneous origin of DNA and proteins. However, for the purpose of this section we will allow that sometime on the early earth the oceans became filled with spontaneously derived DNA.

The question we must now answer is this: Would a DNA molecule that arose by chance possess any information, codes, programs, or instructions?

According to the basic principles of information theory the answer is clearly NO!

The sequence of letters in a book, beads on a string or iron atoms on a computer disc drive, have meaning because the sequences are interpreted within the framework of a pre-existent language convention.

Without a knowledge of the conventions (rules and regulations) which govern information systems or languages, a sequence of letters, beads on a string or dots and dashes, are meaningless.

In all information storage systems the rules and regulations used to interpret sequences must be devised first. Consequently, spontaneously generated letters on a page or nucleotides on a DNA molecule have no meaning (i.e., information) unless rules exist *first*, by which the sequences are interpreted.

Put another way, when we devise a language system we "hang" meaning on the sequence of letters or any information storage medium we choose.

The Monkey and the Typewriter

On June 30, 1860, at the Oxford Union in England, the "Great Debate" occurred between the Anglican Archbishop of Oxford University, Samuel Wilberforce and evolutionist and agnostic, Thomas Huxley.

Bishop Wilberforce, a Professor of Theology and Mathematics at Oxford University, applied the logic of the teleological argument for God. He argued, as did William Paley, that the design we see in nature required a Designer. Therefore, the information (an evidence for design) found in living systems could not arise by chance.

Huxley, on the other hand, declared that given enough time all the possible combinations of matter, including those necessary to produce a man, will eventually occur by chance molecular movement. To prove his point Huxley asked Wilberforce to allow him the service of six monkeys that would live forever, six typewriters that would never wear out and an unlimited supply of paper and ink. He then argued that given an infinite amount of time, according to the Law of Probability, these monkeys would eventually type all of the books in the British Library including the Bible and the works of Shakespeare!

Wilberforce lost the debate because he did not see the flaws in Huxley's argument.

First, the ink from Huxley's typewriters is placed on the paper irreversibly. That is, it types in but it doesn't type out. Chemical reactions in living systems are not this way. They are reversible. In a watery environment, amino acids and nucleotides bond ("type in") and they unbond ("type out"). In fact, they unbond with much greater facility. Consequently, they will have "typed in" as much in 5 billion years as they would in five minutes!

Secondly, because the building blocks of life occur in right and left-handed forms, every other keystroke the monkey strikes (representing the addition of another building block to a DNA or protein molecule) is potentially lethal to the organism! How far do you think the monkey will get with those odds?

In his characteristic style, Sir Fred Hoyle comments on the improbability that Huxley's monkeys might type the genetic code:

No matter how large the environment one considers, life cannot have had a random beginning. Troops of monkeys thundering away at random on typewriters could not produce the works of Shakespeare, for the practical reason that the whole observable universe is not large enough to contain the necessary monkey hordes, the necessary typewriters, and certainly the waste paper baskets required for the deposition of wrong attempts. The same is true for living material.[9]

ET: The Sower of Life?

In the 1970's speculation on the origin of life took an unexpected and bizarre turn. Because the laws of chemistry, physics and mathematical probability so mitigate against the possibility of spontaneous generation, scientists began to look for an extraterrestrial source for the origin of life!

Francis Crick, co-discoverer of DNA, and one of the most respected molecular biologists in the world, has conceded that the spontaneous origin of life on earth is "almost a miracle."

Consequently, since life could not have arisen by chance, he proposed that the first life forms on earth were single-celled "spores" delivered here from interstellar space![10,11] This theory, called "Directed Panspermia," then asserts that these "interstellar spores" subsequently evolved into all the life forms on earth. Similar conclusions were drawn by Hoyle in his book *Evolution from Space*.[12]

This bizarre turn of events begs the question. If we were sprinkled by an extraterrestrial, then who made the ET? Eventually, we must explain the origin of the information on the DNA molecule.

If we speculate that extraterrestrials evolved from primordial goo on another planet and then sprinkled our planet with spores, then we are, in effect, proposing that the laws of physics and chemistry and mathematics are different somewhere else in the universe. That is, we are assuming spontaneous generation did occur somewhere in the universe even though it cannot happen on earth.

If life is of extraterrestrial origin, but the spontaneous generation of highly complex, information rich molecules is impossible anywhere in the universe, then it means that the extraterrestrial source must also be of extra dimensional origin. This means an extra dimensional, supernatural Creator, beyond time and space! Only the Bible teaches the notion of an extra dimensional, transcendent Creator who existed before the creation of the space-time domain.

1   Stanley Miller, Science, Vol. 117 (1953), 528-529.

2   Shapiro, *op cit.*, 99.

3   The Creation Hypothesis. See the Chapter on
    "The Origin of Life," by Thaxton and Bradley.

4   This is detailed in chapter three in *The Creator
    Beyond Time and Space,* Mark Eastman, Chuck
    Missler (Santa Ana, CA: The Word for Today,
    1996).

5   Because of this difficulty some have proposed
    that the origin of life occurred near hot oceanic
    deep sea vents where the water is driven off by
    the the extreme heat. However, this view ignores
    the fact that the heat causes proteins and nucleic
    acids (DNA and RNA) to unfold and breakdown
    as well!

6   Shapiro, *op. cit.*, 108-109.

7   Shapiro, *op. cit.*, 116.

8   *Nature* (November 12, 1981).

9   Sir Fred Hoyle and Chandra Wickramasinghe,
    *Evolution from Space: A Theory of Cosmic
    Creationism* (New York: Simon and Schuster,
    1981), 148.

10 Francis Crick, *Life Itself* (New York: Simon and
    Schuster, 1981).

11 Francis Crick and Leslie Orgel, *Directed
    Panspermia*, Icarus, 19:341-46.

12 Fred Hoyle, *Evolution from Space* (1981).

CHAPTER III

THE ORIGIN OF SPECIES

While a naturalistic explanation for the origin of life is critical to evolutionary purists, Darwin's book, *The Origin of Species*, spent very little time on this issue. Darwin's primary goal was to describe a natural mechanism for the origin of complex structures in living systems as well as the origin of new species themselves.

By the time *Origin* was published naturalists had extensively cataloged and compared thousands of the many life forms on earth. In the eighteenth century, biologists recognized many divisions of organisms that were believed to be distinct interbreeding populations. While world authorities still disagree, the definition of a species is generally understood as a group of organisms that interbreed in the wild. Prior to Darwin's theories most biologists believed that distinct groups of organisms (kingdom, phylum, class, order, family, genus and species) were the result of divine creation. Darwin specifically set out to dispel this very notion.

"Descent With Modification"

Darwin proposed that an organism's inheritable traits were "mutable." By this he meant that they could be changed, either for better or for worse, through a process at that time yet unknown. This mutability provided, according to Darwin, a rich pool of possible traits with which an animal might be born.

According to Darwin those organisms most fit for their environment are more likely to succeed in the competition for resources and therefore survive to the age of reproductive maturity. In turn, those traits will be preferentially passed to the next generation. The fittest organisms were, in effect, "selected" by nature.

Over time the mutability of an organism's traits coupled with such "natural selection," produced entirely new species as well as the highly complex adaptations, i.e., hearts, brains, eyes, kidneys, etc.... Darwin called this process "descent with modification." Providing a possible mechanism for evolution was, in the minds of contemporary biologists, Darwin's greatest contribution.

The Neo-Darwinian Formulation

When the structure of DNA and the method of information storage in living systems was deciphered, the method by which an organism's traits were "mutable" became apparent.

As discussed in chapter two, the information (chemical instructions) for the production of all the structures in all the life-forms on earth is stored by long chains of nucleotides. Two of these chains are bonded together to form the double spiral helix DNA molecule. A section of DNA is produced by adding one nucleotide at a time onto an ever-lengthening chain. From time to time an incorrect nucleotide will be placed resulting in a slightly different "daughter molecule." These errors in replication are called mutations.

With this new understanding of the molecular basis of inheritance, Darwin's theory was reformulated into the "neo-Darwinian synthesis." This new formulation proposes that "beneficial" mutations will increase the "fitness" of an organism increasing the likelihood that it will survive to reproductive maturity and pass those mutations to the next generation.[13]

According to theory, these beneficial mutations are then selected by nature and are concentrated and distributed throughout the population. Over time, natural selection, coupled with millions of "beneficial" mutations, will produce a new species of individuals which are better adapted (i.e., more fit) to the environment they occupy.

From the Goo to You

Darwin's theory proposes that all life on earth began as single-celled organisms similar to the simplest bacteria on earth. Over time these single-celled organisms evolved via the process of mutation and natural selection into all the complex life forms on planet earth.

The simplest free-living bacterial organism (an amoebae) has a genetic blueprint of approximately two million nucleotide pairs. This compares to at least six-billion nucleotide pairs in the forty-six chromosomes found in every human being.

According to the principles of information theory, the information required to create or synthesize a machine is directly related to its complexity. NASA's Space Shuttle is much more complex than a paper airplane. Indeed the amount of information required to produce a Space Shuttle is vastly greater than the amount of information required to produce a paper airplane.

A human being is vastly more complex than a single-celled bacterium. Consequently, much more information is required to construct a man.

If we propose that a single-celled organism developed into a human being then we are, in effect, proposing the spontaneous generation of vast quantities of *new* information. This additional information is required to guide the production of all the complex systems (cardiovascular, visual, respiratory, gastrointestinal and reproductive, etc.) that we humans possess and bacteria do not.

According to neo-Darwinian theory, the information required to change a simple single-celled organism into a man was generated by the chance mutation of an existing genetic program—the one required to produce the single-celled free-living organism in the first place.[14]

However, in recent years the claims of neo-Darwinists that mutations and natural selection are the source of new and beneficial information has been seriously threatened by the science of information theory.

Mutations: The Source of New Information?

Mutations are simply random changes in the nucleotides sequence of a DNA molecule. These errors in copying of DNA are random and non-directional. Because of the error correcting duplication process discussed in chapter two, mutations are very rare.

Regarding the rarity of mutations biologist Francisco Ayala stated;

> *Although mutation is the ultimate source of all genetic variation, it is a relatively rare event.* [15]

Secondly, experimental evidence to date indicates that the vast majority of mutations are either harmful, lethal or at best neutral to an existing code or program. In fact, there are many fatal diseases which are the result of a single genetic mutation. Truly advantageous mutations are extremely rare.

Regarding the nature of mutations scientist C.P. Martin stated;

> *Mutation does produce hereditary changes, but the mass of evidence shows that all, or almost all,*

known mutations are unmistakably pathological and the few remaining ones are highly suspect. [16]

Theodosius Dobzhansky stated;

The process of mutation is the only known source of the raw materials of genetic variability, and hence of evolution...the mutants which arise are, with rare exceptions, deleterious to their carriers, at least in the environments which the species normally encounters. [17]

While it is impossible to know with certainty, it has been estimated that less than one in ten thousand mutations is beneficial to an organism. If this is true, it means that nine thousand, nine hundred, and ninety-nine mutations out of ten thousand are either harmful, lethal or neutral to the population of organisms in question.

While one might imagine that beneficial mutations could accumulate in a given population, it is incredulous to assume that they could do so without the accumulation of many more harmful mutations.

Most lethal mutations will not be passed to the next generation because the organisms that possess them rarely survive to reproductive maturity. However, harmful mutations, which gradually cause the extinction of a species, are passed to the next generation.

Consequently, it is much more likely that a population will become extinct before it is improved by random mutations! This assertion is supported by the principles of information theory.

Codes and programs, such as those found in computer software, are always the result of intelligent design and contrivance. When a software developer attempts to write a code, a program or a language convention, he expends a great amount of time and energy trying to assure that chance plays no role in the formation and function of the code. In fact, when chance errors do occur in the writing of a software program it usually causes the program to malfunction, hence the term "bug." Such bugs are, in effect, the information scientist's equivalent to a mutation in the DNA molecule and the genetic code.

Consequently, when viewed from the point of view of information science, mutations are harmful to existing codes and are, in effect, informational "noise" or static. Because the great abundance of mutations are harmful, lethal or neutral, the amount of static accumulated in the genetic code would far outweigh any beneficial changes in the code and would result in the eventual destruction of the code altogether. In biological systems this means extinction.

Over time, as dictated by the Second Law of Thermodynamics, such informational errors (mutations) in an existing code will cause the code to contain less information and eventually become nonfunctional. The result is the destruction of the code and the death of the organism and the interbreeding population as a whole. This insight has not been adequately addressed by evolutionists to this point.

---

13 *Beneficial*, in Darwinian terms, means a mutation which produces a structural or functional change which increases the chances of survival for an organism's *offspring*. In turn, these offspring live longer and theoretically have more offspring themselves.

14 Some biologists agrue that genetic recombination, over time, can provide additional holistic information. However, the principles of information theory do not allow for such a proposition. Recombination simply "shuffles" existing genetic information in the form of gene packets. It does not create new information.

15 Francisco J. Ayala, "The Mechanisms of Evolution," *Scientific Amencan*, Vol. 239 (September, 1978), 63.

16 C. P. Martin, "A Non-Geneticist Looks at Evolution," *American Scientist* (January 1953), 103.

17   Theodosius Dobzhansky, "On Methods of
     Evolutionary Biology and Anthropology,"
     American Scientist (December 1957), 385.

CHAPTER IV

The Problem of Intermediate Forms

The primary postulate of Darwinian evolution is that interbreeding populations change, over long time periods, into new species which are genetically distinct from their predecessors. For example, it is generally accepted that amphibians evolved into reptiles. Evolutionists also accept that reptiles evolved into birds and mammals over many millions of years.

If this scenario is true then it means that these organisms passed through innumerable intermediate stages on the evolutionary path to a new species. Furthermore, this scenario also demands that complex new systems and structures be developed.

For example, if reptiles evolved into birds then there are a number of new adaptations that had to evolve from previously extant reptile structures. Light-weight bones adapted for flight had to evolve from heavier reptile bones. Wings had to evolve from the forelimbs of a reptile and feathers had to evolve from scales or some other structure in the reptile's skin.

If reptiles evolved into mammals then this means that egg laying was replaced by inter-uterine pregnancy in mammals. Scales were presumably replaced by hair. Finally, mammary glands, for the production of milk, had to evolve from an unknown structure, presumably in the skin.

Such changes are not trivial. They involve major changes in the structure and function of previously extant systems. For this to occur there must be the addition of millions of bits of new information to the genetic code of the ancestral organism.

Darwin knew that if his scenario for evolution was true then there would have been millions of transitional organisms. That is, organisms that were, for example, between a reptile and a bird. Genetically, such organisms would not be considered reptiles anymore. However, they would not be fully bird-like either.

Darwin recognized that if such intermediates ever existed then the record of their existence would be preserved in the fossil record. During Darwin's time, however, there were no fossils that were recognized as truly transitional. Darwin admitted this deficiency and said that if his theory was true then the transitional forms would eventually be found. However, as we will see, not a single truly transitional form has ever been discovered in the fossil record.

The Origin of Complex Systems

In the last forty years astonishing discoveries in molecular biology have demonstrated that living systems possess unparalleled complexity.

According to molecular biologist Michael Denton, a simple amoebae is more complex than any machine made by man, including the Space Shuttle or a super computer.

Although the tiniest bacterial cells are incredibly small, weighing less than 10^{-12} grams, each is in *effect a veritable micro-miniaturized factory containing thousands of exquisitely designed pieces of intricate molecular machinery, made up altogether of one hundred thousand million atoms, far more complicated than any machine built by man and absolutely without parallel in the non-living world.[18]*

Within the structure of a complex machine like the space shuttle we see a variety of interdependent systems. There are the onboard computers for information storage and retrieval. There are systems for maintaining the proper environment inside the cabin. There are systems which function to generate and facilitate the use of energy. There are navigational systems, communication systems, and multiple systems involved in launching and landing the Space Shuttle.

When we examine living systems we find a number of striking parallels to complex machines. In mammals, for example, we find the visual system for processing light, an olfactory system which analyzes chemicals in the air to provide our sense of smell. We have an auditory system for hearing, a respiratory system for the maintenance of proper oxygen balance, a cardiovascular system which delivers oxygen to the entire body. We find waste removal systems such as the kidneys and the liver which cleanse and purify the blood stream.

However, unlike any machine made by man, living systems are capable of self-reproduction. This capability requires a vast amount of additional information storage and complex machinery.

Every one of these systems is a highly complex, machine-like collection of molecular "hardware." In addition, every system in our bodies is composed of multiple sub-systems or integrated parts, each of which is required for the system to function at all. If neo-Darwinian evolution is valid it must explain the origin of these systems without the introduction of intelligent guidance or expertise.

The Eye: Darwin's Nightmare

It is now time to put the creative power of mutation and natural selection to the test. Let's examine, for example, the question of the origin of the human visual system.

The visual system in human beings is an incredibly complex, integrated system which converts photons into meaningful information with incredible speed, unparalleled by modern video digitizing computers. The enormous complexity of vision was eloquently discussed by John Stevens, in *Byte* Magazine, in 1985;

While today's digital hardware is extremely impressive, it is clear that the human retina's real-time performance goes unchallenged. Actually, to simulate 10 milliseconds (ms) of the complete processing of even a single nerve cell from the retina would require the solution of about 500 simultaneous nonlinear differential equations 100 times and would take at least several minutes of processing time on a Cray super computer. Keeping in mind that there are 10 million or more such cells interacting with each other in complex ways, it would take a minimum of 100 years of Cray time to simulate what takes place in your eye many times every second.[19]

In the eye, there is a lens which focuses images on the retina in the back of the eye. On the retina visual images are displayed up-side-down. Within the retina, there is a highly complex chemical system which converts the photons of light to electrons. These electrons then travel down a "wire," the optic nerve, to at least three different areas in the brain.

The visual signal travels first to the geniculate body where the visual information is first organized. The visual signals are then sent to the occipital cortex where the visual information is displayed right-side-up, and finally to the frontal lobes of the brain where pattern recognition occurs.

Unless all of these sub-systems are present and properly connected, the visual system *does not* function. A visual system composed of four-fifths of the necessary components does not give eighty percent vision. It provides no vision at all!

Consequently, one of the most difficult problems for the neo-Darwinian evolutionary theory is to explain how highly complex systems, such as the visual system, which is composed of multiple indispensable sub-systems, could have arisen over a long period of time when a partially evolved system is of no use to the organism.

According to neo-Darwinian theory this occurred by the piecemeal accumulation of mutations necessary to code for each of the sub-components. These sub-components were then integrated and connected, ultimately resulting in a functional visual system.

The Fatal Flaw!

While this scenario may, on the surface, seem reasonable, there is a fatal flaw seldom recognized by evolutionary theorists.

According to evolutionary theory, mutations are preferentially selected, concen-trated and distributed throughout a population when they are beneficial; that is, when they increase the "fitness" of an organism and its offspring.

Consequently, according to neo-Darwinian theory, complex systems, such as the visual system, would have arisen very gradually over millions of years through the step by step accumulation of mutations necessary to produce the separate parts.

However, this mechanism has an insurmountable difficulty which has not been adequately addressed by evolutionists.

According to standard evolutionary thinking, approximately 800 million years ago a blind primitive creature had a number of mutations which gave rise to a pigmented spot on the surface of its skin. This pigmented spot was the beginning of an early retina. Gradually, the pigmented cells became connected to a nerve which in turn became connected to the organism's brain. Over many millions of years all the various parts of this primitive visual system became connected and the organism could sense light. Evolutionists admit that such early visual systems could only distinguish between light and dark. However, this newly developed ability gave the organism a competitive advantage over its neighbors and, therefore, it was more successful in competing for resources.

The problem with this theory is that the mutations that gave rise to the early eye will provide no increased functional capacity to the organism. This is because a partially evolved visual system does not provide a little bit of vision, it provides no vision at all. Consequently, the mutations that produced the primitive eye (the pigmented spot) will not be beneficial and will not be concentrated in the population. They will be lost and the fortuitous genetic experiment to create vision will be a bust!

The fundamental failure of mutation and natural selection, as presented by the neo-Darwinists, is that there is no known mechanism which will allow the mutations that produce one of the sub-systems in the visual system to wait around for millions of years while the other sub-systems are being produced in a similar piece-meal random fashion.

Arthur Koestler comments on the implausibility of this scenario;

> Each mutation occurring alone would be wiped out before it could be combined with the others. They are all inter-dependent. The doctrine that their coming together was due to a series of blind coincidences is an affront not only to common sense but to the basic principles of scientific explanation.[20]

Charles Darwin even admitted that his theory was insufficient to explain the origin of complex systems such as the visual system;

> *To suppose that the eye with all its inimitable contrivances for adjusting the focus to different distances, for admitting different amounts of light, and for the correction of spherical and chromatic aberration, could have been formed by natural selection, seems, I freely confess, absurd in the highest degree.*[21]

The point is that a transitional visual system, i.e., one which is on the way to being produced, is impossible to visualize from a neo-Darwinian point of view. This dilemma has also been recognized by a number of scientists in recent decades;

> *The eye, as one of the most complex organs, has been the symbol and archetype of his [Darwin's] dilemma. Since the eye is obviously of no use at all except in its final, complete form, how could natural selection have functioned in those initial stages of its evolution when the variations had no possible survival value? No single variation, indeed no single part, being of any use without every other, and natural selection presuming no knowledge of the ultimate end or purpose of the organ, the criterion of utility, or survival, would seem to be irrelevant. And there are other equally provoking examples of organs and processes*

which seem to defy natural selection. Biochemistry provides the case of chemical synthesis built up in several stages, of which the intermediate substance formed at any one stage is of no value at all, and only the end product, the final elaborate and delicate machinery, is useful— and not only useful but vital to life. How can selection, knowing nothing of the end or final purpose of this process, function when the only test is precisely that end or final purpose?[22]

If we assume that life is the product of intelligent design we can see that the designer need only place all of the sub-components together in the organism simultaneously and they would be fully functional. On this point, neo-Darwinism fails entirely to explain the origin of complex systems.

If this were not enough we now know that the complex systems in organisms such as human beings are also integrated. For example, the visual system is connected to the digestive system. When we see a photograph of a food we like, we begin to salivate. The respiratory and the cardiovascular system are connected to the visual system, endocrine system, to the reproductive system and on and on.

Each of the systems affects the other systems in ways that insure the survival and preservation of the species. It staggers the mind to imagine how such complex systems could be built in a piecemeal fashion over millions of years by the neo-Darwinian evolutionary process.

Robert Jastrow echoed this sentiment when he stated;

> *It is hard to accept the evolution of the human eye as a product of chance; it is even harder to accept the evolution of human intelligence as the product of random disruptions in the brain cells of our ancestors.*[23]

Try To Imagine...?

When the deficiencies of mutations are pointed out, evolutionists usually bring up their second and most powerful creative force, natural selection.

Natural selection, as we have discussed, is the "blind" selection of those traits which are most favored for a particular environment. For example, in a very cold environment those organisms with a thick coat of fur and a thick layer of fat will be more fit than a hairless, thin creature.

However, traits which are favorable to one environment may be extremely detrimental to a species in another environment. Those organisms which have the most ideal collection of traits for their environment are said to be the "fittest."

The environment does not consciously select the traits that are most fit. It is simply the fact that those organisms which possess a collection of traits that allows them to survive to reproductive maturity are considered most fit.

So natural selection does not create anything. Nature simply preserves favorable traits that are already present in the breeding population.

In an article in *Science*, a prestigious secular journal committed to the promotion of evolution, biologist Daniel Brooks stated;

> [Natural selection] may have a stabilizing effect, but it does not promote speciation. It is not a creative force as many people have suggested.[24]

A simple illustration will help us understand this major deficiency of natural selection.

Let's examine the notion of natural selection and the origin of flight. According to evolutionists, birds evolved from a reptile-like creature some 60-100 million years ago. Evolutionists propose that the forelimb of the reptile evolved into wings as the scales were gradually transformed into feathers. This process, taking millions of years, occurred as random mutations caused the scales of the reptile to be gradually lengthened. Eventually, the scales were converted to fully developed feathers and flight emerged.

On the surface, this scenario may seem reasonable. However, the supposed creative force of natural selection is, in fact, a tremendous stumbling block to the evolution of flight. An illustration will help to drive home the point.

Imagine a population of lizards that are highly skilled in running and hunting. Then one day a "litter" of lizards is hatched who have, in their genetic code, a mutation that caused their scales to be four times longer than normal. At this point the lizards cannot fly because the scales do not provide any significant aerodynamic lift.

These lizards, in turn have offspring which have an additional mutation which lengthens the scales even further. From an evolutionary viewpoint the scales are well on their way to evolving into feathers.

Over the next 1,000 generations hundreds of additional mutations occur which cause further lengthening of the scales. The scales are now about half the size necessary to allow for flight. However, there is a problem.

The long stiff scales now begin to hinder the lizards ability to run and climb. As the scales continue to lengthen in succeeding generations the problem worsens.

What was once a swift runner and climber has become a clumsy creature that cannot run nor climb as well as its adversaries. So natural selection, which allows for the "survival of the fittest," becomes the enemy of this transitional form.

Since it cannot run as it once did, this transitional form cannot catch its prey as efficiently as a true lizard. And because it cannot climb as well as it once could, it cannot evade its predators. So it loses out in the competition for resources or is killed by its fleet-footed predators. Natural selection then wipes out the evolutionary experiment because it is not as fit as its predecessors or its competition.

The point is that the lizard's forelimb becomes a "bad leg" long before it becomes a "good wing." So the transitional form is eliminated by natural selection because it is less fit. Natural selection, therefore, tends to be a preserving force rather than a creative force.

Many other examples like this could be imagined where a transitional structure is less fit than its predecessor.

How would a transitional reproductive system function? Unless all the parts are present and fully functional it does not work. How would a transitional ear perceive sound? Unless all the parts are connected and functioning properly, the auditory system does not function.

This inability to conceive of transitional structures has rarely been addressed by evolutionists. Those that have addressed it have expressed their frustration about this problem.

Stephen Jay Gould, professor of paleontology at Harvard University addressed the problem of the viability of transitional structures;

> *Of what possible use are the imperfect incipient stages of useful structures? What good is half a jaw or half a wing?*[25]

Some will argue that organisms, like the Horseshoe Crab, have a "transitional visual system" which is an early evolutionary stage of our own visual system. However, what they fail to recognize is that the Horseshoe Crab's visual system possesses all of the basic parts of the mammalian visual system. That is, it possesses a lens to focus an image, a retina to convert photons to electrons, an optic nerve to send the electrons to the brain and the necessary connections in the brain to make sense of the visual information.

Far from being a primitive system, the Horseshoe Crab's visual system is, in principle, as complex as the human visual system and is in no way a "transitional" visual system. It is fully functional and fully integrated.

The Fossil Record

When Charles Darwin wrote *The Origin of Species*, he knew that if his theory was true the record of evolution should be found throughout the earth in the sedimentary rocks. However, by Darwin's time tens of thousands of fossils had been found which revealed the skeletal structure of hundreds of different species. However, Darwin himself admitted that the fossil record did not support his theory.

> But, as by this theory innumerable transitional forms must have existed, why do we not find them imbedded in countless numbers in the crust of the earth?[26]

> The number of intermediate varieties, which have formerly existed [must] truly be enormous. Why then is not every geological formation and every stratum full of such intermediate links? Geology assuredly does not reveal any such finely-graduated organic chain; and this, perhaps, is the

> *most obvious and serious objection which can be*
> *urged against the theory [of evolution].*[27]

Nearly 150 years later the situation hasn't changed. World authorities still agree that the fossil record does not support the gradual evolution of life on earth.

> *Well, we are now about 120 years after Darwin*
> *and the knowledge of the fossil record has been*
> *greatly expanded. We now have a quarter of a*
> *million fossil species but the situation hasn't*
> *changed much. The record of evolution is still*
> *surprisingly jerky and, ironically, we have even*
> *fewer examples of evolutionary transition than*
> *we had in Darwin's time.*[28]

Finally, in the late 1970's, Stephen Jay Gould confirmed the fact that the fossil record does not confirm the process of evolution.

> *The extreme rarity of transitional forms in the*
> *fossil record persists as the trade secret of*
> *paleontology. The evolutionary trees that adorn*
> *our textbooks have data only at the tips and nodes*
> *of their branches; the rest is inference. However*
> *reasonable, not the evidence of fossils…. We*
> *fancy ourselves as the only true students of life's*
> *history, yet to preserve our favored account of*
> *evolution by natural selection we view our data*
> *as so bad that we never see the very process we*
> *profess to study.*[29]

In other words, the evolutionary trees "that adorn our textbooks" are based on conjecture, i.e., they guessed.

Made by Design!

In this brief review of Darwinian evolutionary theory we have seen that the "mutability" of inherited traits, coupled with natural selection, is totally incapable of explaining the origin of the complex, integrated systems found in living organisms. Chance chemistry, the god of Darwinian evolution, is also incapable of explaining the origin of life. So the question remains; how did the incredibly complex structures found in living systems arise?

As we have seen, the fundamental error of Darwinism is the non-viability of transitional systems. Unless the sub-components of complex systems arise simultaneously they will not function. As a result, the mutations that gave rise to the primitive sub-components will be lost and will not be preserved and concentrated in the population. However, the only other option to the chance origin of complex systems is that their sub-components were intentionally designed and brought together as an act of purposeful creation. There is no third option.

Since the laws of chemistry and physics in our universe are incapable of explaining the chance origin and evolution of life then the source must be an extra dimensional one. That is, a creative source that exists outside time and space.

For thousands of years the Bible has taught that God is a transcendent Being who existed before time and space and spoke the universe and its life forms into existence. In Isaiah 57:15 we are told that God inhabits eternity, a domain outside time and space;

> For thus says the High and Lofty One Who inhabits eternity, whose name is Holy: "I dwell in the high and holy place, with him who has a contrite and humble spirit, to revive the spirit of the humble, and to revive the heart of the contrite ones."

The Bible also teaches that time, space and matter had a beginning in Genesis 1:1;

> In the beginning God created the heavens and the earth.

Remarkably, in the twentieth century astronomers have arrived at the same conclusion: Time, space and matter had a beginning.[30]

It is indeed ironic that twentieth century scientific inquiry now demands a Creator that exists outside the space-time domain; One that "inhabits eternity." The Creator revealed in the Bible is not only outside time and space, according to the biblical account, that Creator applied biochemical know-how onto matter and designed and created man from "the dust of the earth."

Paul the Apostle said in Romans chapter one that the existence of God is confirmed in the things that are made. Indeed, the Creator revealed in the Bible has revealed Himself to mankind through His Creation, through His Word and through His Son Jesus Christ. The Bible teaches that Jesus Christ is the very Creator of the universe who, though He inhabited eternity, became flesh and dwelt among us. The One who provided a way of salvation through His substitutionary, sacrificial death on a cross nearly 2,000 years ago. By faith in Him and Him alone we can have forgiveness of our sins, reconciliation with our Creator and eternal life in heaven with Him "Who inhabits eternity... whose name is Holy."

---

18 Michael Denton, *Evolution: A Theory in Crisis* (Adler and Adler, 1986), 250.

19 John K. Stevens, "Reverse Engineering the Brain," *Byte* (April 1985), 287.

20   Arthur Koestler, *The Ghost in the Machine* (New York: Macmillan Publishing Co., 1968), 129.

21   Charles Darwin, *The Origin of Species*, 75.

22   Gertrude Himmelfarb, *Darwin and the Darwinian Revolution* (Doubleday, 1959), 320-321.

23   Robert Jastrow, "Evolution: Selection for Perfection," *Science Digest* (December 1981), 87.

24   Daniel Brooks, as quoted by Roger Lewin, "A Downward Slope to Greater Diversity," *Science*, Vol. 217. 24 (September 1982), 124Q.

25   Stephen Jay Gould, "The Return of Hopeful Monsters," *Natural History*, Vol. 86 (June-July 1977), 23.

26   Darwin, *The Origin of Species*, 163.

27   Ibid, p. 323.

28   David M. Raup, "Conflicts Between Darwin and Paleontology," Field Museum of Natural History Bulletin, Vol. 50, No. 1 (January 1979), 25.

29   Stephen Jay Gould, "Evolution's Erratic Pace," *Natural History*, Vol. 5 (May 1977), 14.

30   See *The Creator Beyond Time and Space*, Chapter 2, Mark Eastman, Chuck Missler (The Word for Today, 714-979-0706).

How to Become a Christian

First of all you must recognize that you are a sinner. Realize that you have missed the mark. This is true of each of us. We have deliberately crossed the line not once, but many times. The Bible says, *"All have sinned and fallen short of the glory of God"* (Romans 3:23). This is a hard admission for many to make, but if we are not willing to hear the bad news, we cannot appreciate and respond to the *good news*.

Second, we must realize that Jesus Christ died on the cross for us. Because of sin, God had to take drastic measures to reach us. So He came to this earth and walked here as a man. But Jesus was more than just a good man. He was the God-man—God incarnate—and that is why His death on the cross is so significant.

At the cross, God Himself—in the person of Jesus Christ—took our place and bore our sins. He paid for them and purchased our redemption.

Third, we must repent of our sin. God has commanded men everywhere to repent. Acts 3:19 states, *"Repent therefore and be converted, that your sins may be blotted out, so that times of refreshing may come from the presence of the Lord."* What does this word *repent* mean? It means to change direction–to hang a U-turn on the road of life. It means to stop living the kind of life we led previously and start living the kind of life outlined in the pages of the Bible. Now we must change and be willing to make a break with the past.

Fourth, we must receive Jesus Christ into our hearts and lives. Being a Christian is having God Himself take residence in our lives. John 1:12 tells us, *"But as many as received Him, to them He gave the right to become children of God."* We must receive Him. Jesus said, *"Behold, I stand at the door and knock. If anyone hears My voice and opens the door, I will come in..."* (Revelation 3:20). Each one of us must individually decide to open the door. How do we open it? Through prayer.

If you have never asked Jesus Christ to come into your life, you can do it right now. Here is a suggested prayer you might even pray.

Lord Jesus, I know that I am a sinner and I am sorry for my sin. I turn and repent of my sins right now. Thank You for dying on the cross for me and paying the price for my sin. Please come into my heart and life right now. Fill me with Your Holy Spirit and help me to be Your disciple. Thank You for forgiving me and coming into my life. Thank You that I am now a child of Yours and that I am going to heaven. In Jesus' name, I pray. Amen.

When you pray that prayer God will respond. You have made the right decision–the decision that will impact how you spend eternity. Now you will go to heaven, and in the meantime, find peace and the answers to your spiritual questions.

Taken from: *Life. Any Questions?*
by Greg Laurie, Copyright © 1995. Used by permission.

Other books available in this series...

Spiritual Warfare
by Brian Brodersen
Pastor Brian Brodersen of Calvary Chapel Westminster, England brings biblical balance and practical insight to the subject of spiritual warfare.

Christian Leadership
by Larry Taylor
Pastor Larry Taylor of the Cornerstone Christian Fellowship in Maui, Hawaii discusses the basics of leadership in the church and challenges us to become leaders that serve.

The Psychologizing of the Faith
by Bob Hoekstra
Pastor Bob Hoekstra of Living in Christ Ministries calls the church to leave the broken cisterns of human wisdom, and to return to the fountain of living water flowing from our wonderful counselor, Jesus Christ.

Practical Christian Living
by Wayne Taylor
Pastor Wayne Taylor of Calvary Fellowship in Seattle, Washington takes us through a study of Romans 12 and 13 showing us what practical Christian living is all about.

Building Godly Character
by Ray Bentley

Pastor Ray Bentley of Maranatha Chapel in San Diego, California takes us through a study in the life of David to show how God builds His character in our individual lives.

Worship and Music Ministry
by Rick Ryan & Dave Newton

Pastor Rick Ryan and Dave Newton of Calvary Chapel Santa Barbara, California give us solid biblical insight into the very important subjects of worship and ministering to the body of Christ through music.

Overcoming Sin & Enjoying God
by Danny Bond

Pastor Danny Bond of Pacific Hills Church in Aliso Viejo, California shows us, through practical principles, that it is possible to live in victory over sin and have constant fellowship with our loving God.

Answers for the Skeptic
by Scott Richards

Pastor Scott Richards of Calvary Fellowship in Tucson, Arizona shows us what to say when our faith is challenged, and how to answer the skeptic in a way that opens hearts to the love and truth of Jesus Christ.

Effective Prayer Life
by Chuck Smith

Pastor Chuck Smith of Calvary Chapel of Costa Mesa, California discusses the principles of prayer, the keys to having a dynamic prayer life, and the victorious results of such a life. It will stir in your heart a desire to "pray without ceasing."

Creation by Design
by Mark Eastman, M.D.

Mark Eastman, M.D., of Genesis Outreach in Temecula, California carefully examines and clarifies the evidence for a Creator God, and the reality of His relationship to mankind.

Afterglow
by Henry Gainey

Pastor Henry Gainey of Calvary Chapel Thomasville, Georgia gives instruction in conducting and understanding the proper use of the gifts of the Holy Spirit in an "Afterglow Service."

For ordering information, please contact:
The Word For Today
P.O. Box 8000, Costa Mesa, CA 92628
(800) 272-WORD
Also, visit us on the Internet at:
www.thewordfortoday.org